Personal, Learning & Thinking Skills in PSHE

Creative Thinkers

Eileen Osborne & Steph Yates

Folens

© 2009 Folens Limited, on behalf of the authors.

United Kingdom: Folens Publishers, Waterslade House, Thame Road, Haddenham, Buckinghamshire, HP17 8NT.
Email: folens@folens.com Website: www.folens.com

Ireland: Folens Publishers, Greenhills Road, Tallaght, Dublin 24.
Email: info@folens.ie Website: www.folens.ie

Editor: Louise Clark
Series designer and layout: Fiona Webb
Illustrations: Catherine Ward
Cover design: Form (www.form.uk.com)

The websites recommended in this publication were correct at the time of going to press, however websites may have been removed or web addresses changed since that time. Folens has made every attempt to suggest websites that are reliable and appropriate for student's use. It is not unknown for unscrupulous individuals to put unsuitable material on websites that may be accessed by students. Teachers should check all websites before allowing students to access them. Folens is not responsible for the content of external websites.

For general spellings Folens adheres to *Oxford Dictionary of English*, Second Edition (Revised), 2005.

First published 2009 by Folens Limited.

Every effort has been made to contact copyright holders of material used in this publication. If any copyright holder has been overlooked, we will be pleased to make any necessary arrangements.

British Library Cataloguing in Publication Data. A catalogue record for this publication is available from the British Library.

ISBN 978-1-85008-450-1   Folens code FD4501

Contents

'The personal, learning and thinking skills (PLTS) framework supports young people in their learning across the curriculum. The skills should be developed through a range of experiences and subject contexts.'

(QCA)

This series, PLTS in PSHE, uses the PLTS framework as a linking bridge to the PSHE programmes of study. It provides a context for PSHE departments to contribute to the overall PLTS skills and competencies, and in doing so provides students with the ability to transfer what they have learnt in PSHE across other curriculum areas.

This is one of six books in the series and each book links to one of the six groups of skills in the PLTS framework. This book has as its focus 'creative thinkers'.

CREATIVE THINKERS

Focus

Young people think creatively by generating and exploring ideas, making original connections. They try different ways to tackle a problem, working with others to find imaginative solutions and outcomes that are of value.

Skills, behaviours and personal qualities

Young people:
- generate ideas and explore possibilities
- ask questions to extend their thinking
- connect their own and others' ideas and experiences in inventive ways
- question their own and others' assumptions
- try out alternatives or new solutions and follow ideas through
- adapt ideas as circumstances change.

© Qualifications and Curriculum Authority

Throughout the book students are encouraged to think creatively by generating and exploring ideas and making original connections. They are encouraged to look at different ways of tackling problems while working with others to find solutions which are imaginative and outcomes which are valuable. One important aspect of *Creative Thinkers* is that students learn to question their own and others' assumptions and adapt ideas as circumstances change. This book is divided into units for Key Stage 3 and Key Stage 4.

Teacher's notes

Each unit has accompanying Teacher's Notes which give information on the unit, and ideas on how to use the Activity Sheets, starter activities and plenaries. Each unit has its own set of objectives set out in the Teacher's Notes.

Assessment/Progress sheets

On pages 6–7 there are two sheets which focus on student progress and learning. The two sheets can be used to assess progress, decide on targets and help students to move to a higher level in their learning.

	Unit 1: The real me!	Unit 2: A healthy life?	Unit 3: Relationships (KS3)	Unit 4: Financial matters	Unit 5: Tackling a disaster	Unit 6: Healthy lifestyles	Unit 7: Relationships (KS4)	Unit 8: The alternative prom	Unit 9: Financial management	Unit 10: Where else?
PSHE Programmes of Study for England	Personal wellbeing: 1.1 Personal identities	Personal wellbeing: 1.1 Personal identities; 1.2 Healthy lifestyles	Personal wellbeing: 1.1 Personal identities; 1.3 Risk; 1.4: Relationships	Personal wellbeing: 1.1 Personal identities; Economic wellbeing and financial capability: 1.2 Capability; 1.3 Risk; 1.4 Economic understanding	Personal wellbeing: 1.1 Personal identities; 1.3 Risk; 1.5 Diversity Economic wellbeing and financial capability: 1.3 Risk; 1.4 Economic understanding	Personal wellbeing: 1.1 Personal identities; 1.2 Healthy lifestyles; 1.3 Risk; 1.4: Relationships	Personal wellbeing: 1.1 Personal identities; 1.2 Healthy lifestyles; 1.3 Risk; 1.4: Relationships; 1.5 Diversity	Personal wellbeing: 1.1 Personal identities; 1.3 Risk Economic wellbeing and financial capability: 1.2 Capability	Personal Wellbeing: 1.1 Personal identities; 1.2 Healthy Lifestyles; 1.3 Risk; 1.4 Relationships Economic wellbeing and financial capability: 1.2 Capability	Personal Wellbeing: 1.1 Personal identities; 1.3 Risk; 1.4 Relationships.
Curriculum for Excellence for Scotland	Health and wellbeing: Mental, emotional, social and physical wellbeing	Health and wellbeing: Mental, emotional, social and physical wellbeing	Health and wellbeing: Mental, emotional, social and physical wellbeing; Relationships, sexual health and parenthood	Health and wellbeing: Mental, emotional, social and physical wellbeing	Health and wellbeing: Mental, emotional, social and physical wellbeing	Health and wellbeing: Mental, emotional, social and physical wellbeing; Relationships, sexual health and parenthood	Health and wellbeing: Mental, emotional, social and physical wellbeing; Relationships, sexual health and parenthood	Health and wellbeing: Mental, emotional, social and physical wellbeing	Health and wellbeing: Mental, emotional, social and physical wellbeing	Health and wellbeing: Mental, emotional, social and physical wellbeing; Planning for choices and changes
Personal and Social Education Framework for Wales	Health and emotional wellbeing	Health and emotional wellbeing	Health and emotional wellbeing	Active citizenship	Personal development; Local and global citizenship	Health and emotional wellbeing; Moral and spiritual development	Health and emotional wellbeing; Moral and spiritual development	Health and emotional wellbeing; Active citizenship; Moral and spiritual development	Health and emotional wellbeing; Active citizenship; Moral and spiritual development	Active citizenship
Revised Curriculum for Northern Ireland: Learning for Life and Work	Learning for life and work: Personal development	Learning for life and work: Personal development	Learning for life and work: Personal development	Learning for life and work: Employability	Learning for life and work: Personal development; Local and global citizenship	Learning for life and work: Personal development	Learning for life and work: Personal development	Learning for life and work: Personal development; Local and global citizenship	Learning for life and work: Personal development; Local and global citizenship; Employability	Learning for life and work: Personal development; Employability
Every Child Matters	Make a positive contribution	Be healthy	Be healthy; Stay safe	Achieve economic wellbeing	Make a positive contribution	Be healthy; Stay safe	Be healthy; Stay safe	Make a positive contribution	Achieve economic wellbeing	Enjoy and achieve
Social and Emotional Aspects of Learning	Social skills: Managing feelings	Social skills: Managing feelings	Social skills: Managing feelings	Social skills	Social skills: Empathy	Social skills: Self-awareness	Social skills: Self-awareness	Social skills	Social skills: Empathy	Self-awareness

Creative Thinkers

Tick the boxes to show what applies to you at the start of the unit and then again at the end.

I can...

	At the start of this unit			At the end of this unit		
	🙂	😐	☹️	🙂	😐	☹️
◎ generate ideas						
◎ explore possibilities						
◎ ask questions to extend my thinking						
◎ connect my own and others' ideas and experiences in inventive ways						
◎ question my own assumptions						
◎ question the assumptions of others						
◎ try out alternatives or new solutions						
◎ follow ideas through						
◎ adapt ideas as circumstances change						

My targets at the end of this unit are:

1 _____

_____

2 _____

_____

3 _____

_____

PLTS in PSHE: Creative Thinkers

Creative Thinkers

You have now assessed how creative a thinker you are. This sheet is for you to see how you can progress and improve in the skills needed to be a creative thinker. Each statement indicates what you should do to move to being a good or an excellent creative thinker.

◎ **I can generate ideas.**
I must make sure I know and understand the topic or issue we are looking at.
I must 'think outside the box'.

◎ **I can explore possibilities.**
I must make sure I do not close my mind to possibilities.
I must accept that there may be possibilities which will challenge how I think.

◎ **I can ask questions to extend my thinking.**
I must understand that closed questions are not always the best ones to ask.
I must learn to ask questions which go beyond my understanding.

◎ **I can convey my own and others' ideas and experiences in inventive ways.**
I must understand that there are many different ways to convey ideas and experiences.
I must understand that being inventive might take me outside my 'comfort zone'.

◎ **I can question my own assumptions.**
I must understand that I am not always right in my assumptions.
I must have confidence in my ability to question my assumptions.

◎ **I can question the assumptions of others.**
I must understand that others are not always correct in their assumptions.
I must learn to question the assumptions of others in a non-critical way.

◎ **I can try out alternatives or new solutions.**
I must understand that there are always alternatives or new solutions.
I must learn to step out into the unknown and try out these alternatives or new solutions.

◎ **I can follow ideas through.**
I must learn to commit to my ideas.
I must accept that even though it might be time consuming and difficult, I must follow ideas through.

◎ **I can adapt ideas as circumstances change.**
I must understand ideas may need to be adapted in the face of change.
I must use my skills to understand when to adapt ideas and when to leave them.

Teacher's Notes

Objectives

By the end of the lesson, students will:

◎ understand the main factors which contribute towards personal identity.

◎ understand that everyone has different 'faces' which they use on different occasions.

◎ understand the need to ask questions to extend their thinking.

◎ be able to connect their own and others' ideas and experiences in inventive ways.

Prior knowledge

None.

Links

Personal, Social, Health and Economic Education Programmes of Study for England: Personal Wellbeing: 1.1 Personal identities.

Curriculum for Excellence for Scotland: Health and Wellbeing: Mental, emotional, social and physical wellbeing.

Personal and Social Education Framework for Wales: Health and emotional wellbeing.

Revised Curriculum for Northern Ireland: Learning for Life and Work: Personal development.

Background

Understanding oneself and knowing what kind of person you really are can be the two most profound influences on young people and their future lives and opportunities. Many young people fight shy of understanding themselves and what makes them 'tick' while at the same time they look critically at their peers.

Starter activity

Ask students to list what they think are their three most important skills/qualities – use stick-it notes for this. Students should then put the notes onto the wall or board without showing them to any other student. Invite the class to identify who the descriptions belong to and write the name onto the stick-it note. Discuss whether or not everyone has been correctly identified. Lead from this into how well we know ourselves and each other.

Activity sheets

Activity sheet **1.1 Who Am I?** should first be discussed and students should be prompted to think about what factors make them unique. The sheet should then be completed individually with students ticking those factors they agree with and adding five factors of their own to the grid. Once they have completed the sheet individually it should lead to a discussion about what they have added to the list and how they think their factors are important. It should be stressed that no one factor nor indeed any combination of factors can totally account for the kind of person they eventually become.

Activity sheet **1.2 The 'Inside' Me** should be completed in conjunction with Activity sheet **1.3 The 'Outside' Me** so that students can build up a personal picture of what they are like. When these are completed they can be displayed side by side so that others in the class can look at the sheets and assess whether or not a 'true' picture has been painted.

Activity sheet **1.4 Being Positive About Myself** should be completed individually and students should be reassured that they will not be asked to read out what they have written.

Activity sheet **1.5 I Am ... I Could Be ...** uses the work carried out on the previous Activity sheets. Tell students that this sheet requires them to be very honest about themselves. If students need more space to write in they could use the other side of the sheet. They should look at what they want to change about themselves if they are to have successful lives and what they will have to do in order to effect the changes. You could discuss what is meant by 'a successful life' and how it does not necessarily mean the same thing to everyone.

Plenary

Talk about what the students have learned about themselves. Were they surprised at anything? Did they discover many areas that they thought needed to be changed?

1.1 Who Am I?

Who are you and what makes you you? There are many factors which link to your personal identity. Ten factors are listed below. Tick those you agree with and then add another five of your own.

? ? ? ? ? ? ? ? ? ? ? = ME!

What your family is like	What your friends are like	Whether you are a boy or a girl
Which schools you have gone to	Where you live	How much money your family has
Education level of parents/carers	Age of parents/carers	Jobs of parents/carers
Whether or not you read lots of books		

1.2 The 'Inside' Me

Everyone is at least two different people. There is the 'inside' person and the 'outside' person. This sheet asks you to focus on your inside person. You should write inside the body shape all those things that make up the kind of person you are but which cannot be seen with the naked eye, e.g. your personality, inherited characteristics, intelligence, fears, hopes, etc. You should create a true picture of the inside you!

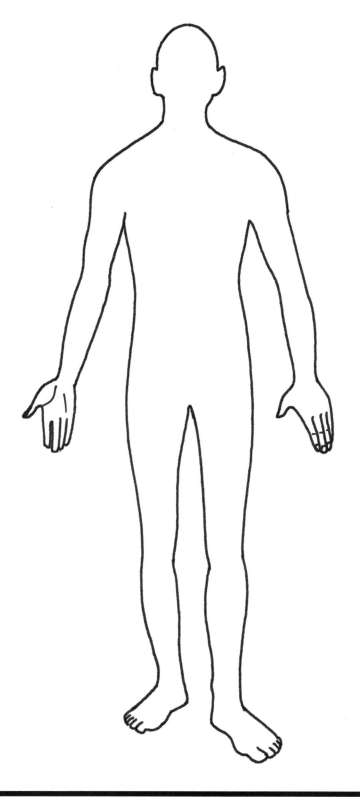

PLTS in PSHE: Creative Thinkers © Folens (copiable page)

1.3 The 'Outside' Me

This sheet asks you to describe the 'outside' you, i.e. what others can see and how you might appear to others. Around the question mark you should write what others can see about you, e.g. hair colour, and also how you might appear to others even though you may not really be like that, e.g. friendly even though you know it takes a lot for you to be friendly.

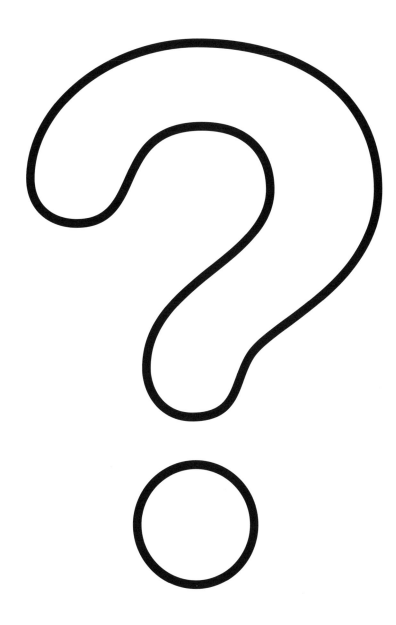

1.4 Being Positive About Myself

How confident are you? Can you stand up for yourself? Are you able to push your ideas forward if you need to? Do you feel good about yourself?

Complete the sentences below.

I feel confident when …

I can stand up for myself when …

I can push my ideas forward when …

I feel good about myself when …

PLTS in PSHE: Creative Thinkers

1.5 I Am ... I Could Be ...

Read through your completed Activity sheets 1.1–1.4 to remind yourself what you wrote. If someone else read them would they recognise you? Would they agree with what you have said about yourself? Have you been truthful about yourself? Now you are going to ask questions about yourself and decide on the elements of yourself you could change in order to be a very successful adult. In the first column write down the top five things about yourself that you would not want to change. In the middle column write down the top five things about yourself you would change if you could. In the last column write down what you will have to do to make sure you change. Remember – anything is possible!

I want to keep:	I want to change:	This is what I have to do to change:

Objectives

By the end of the lesson, students will:

◎ understand what it means to lead a 'healthy life'.

◎ understand the links between a 'healthy life' and physical, emotional, mental and sexual health.

◎ be able to generate ideas and explore different possibilities.

◎ be able to question their own and others' assumptions.

Prior knowledge

None.

Links

Personal, Social, Health and Economic Education Programmes of Study for England: Personal Wellbeing: 1.1 Personal identities; 1.2 Healthy lifestyles.

Curriculum for Excellence for Scotland: Health and Wellbeing: Mental, emotional, social and physical wellbeing.

Personal and Social Education Framework for Wales: Health and emotional wellbeing.

Revised Curriculum for Northern Ireland: Learning for Life and Work: Personal development.

Background

In recent years many comments have been made about the fact that 'children grow up too quickly'. For girls, puberty can happen at an early age, sometimes nine-years-old or even younger, while parenthood can be as early as 11- or 12-years-old. However, growing up is not just about puberty and body changes. It is also about the maturation of mental and emotional health, and the understanding of sexuality, and linking all these factors together to make sure the individual has a 'healthy life'.

Many adults do not make the link between emotional and mental health and being healthy, and young people can sometimes also fail to make the connections. The concept of the 'whole person' has come more and more into the public focus and young people should be aware of how the different elements affect them as individuals and society as a whole.

Starter activity

Talk about how you can identify a child, e.g. what does a child look like? How does a child act and think? How can you tell when a child is changing into a young person?

Activity sheets

On Activity sheet **2.1 What Does 'Growing Up' Mean?** students are asked to read comments from various individuals and then write down their own definition of the phrase 'growing up'. You could read through the statements and discuss each one before the students write their own definitions down. Once students have written their definitions you should spend time discussing what they have said. You could extend the discussion to look at whether or not it is always a good thing to 'grow up' and what society expects 'grown ups' to be like.

Activity sheets **2.2–2.5** are all linked and ask students to define physical, mental, sexual and emotional health. The sheets then lead on to look at what else the students would like to know about that aspect of health, and end by developing their understanding of the meaning of good/bad in relation to the four aspects. These four sheets should be discussed and a class consensus reached as to the definitions for each aspect and what implications they have for health. Care should be taken when looking at the four aspects with regard to Child Protection disclosures and other intimate disclosures.

Activity sheet **2.6 What Does It Mean?** looks at assumptions students might have made in connection with the four aspects of health that have been examined and then requires students to suggest initiatives or alternatives to existing initiatives to help young people to become more healthy.

Plenary

Look at why the government is keen to make the nation healthier. What are the problems an unhealthy nation can cause?

2.1 What Does 'Growing Up' Mean?

Read how the people below define 'growing up' and then write your own definition of it.

Tom, aged 14: I never want to grow up because you become old and boring and never have any real fun.

Matt, aged 67: My children say to me "Oh, grow up Dad" and I say "Why?".

Abbie, aged 23: I was pleased to grow up because I hated being a child and not being able to do so many things.

Masood, aged 30: Growing up means body changes, mental changes and accepting responsibility for your actions. It means having a job and looking after yourself.

Ron, aged 19: I had to grow up quick because my parents died in a car crash. Growing up isn't all it's cracked up to be.

Chris, aged 40: It's all about changing and becoming an adult and you can't stop that process. I would argue that some people never really grow up because it is also about being your own person and some adults can't really do that.

For me 'growing up' means …

2.2 Physical Health

In small groups discuss what the term 'physical health' means. Once you have decided on your definition write it in the space provided. Then write down four questions you would like to ask to extend your knowledge and understanding of physical health. Finally, write down what assumptions you might make about someone who is in poor physical health.

Physical health means ...

Four questions we would ask:

1

2

3

4

Being in poor physical health would mean ...

2.3 Mental Health

In small groups discuss what the term 'mental health' means. Once you have decided on your definition write it in the space provided. Then write down four questions you would like to ask to extend your knowledge and understanding of mental health. Finally, write down what assumptions you might make about someone who is in poor mental health.

Mental health means ...

Four questions we would ask:

1

2

3

4

Being in poor mental health would mean ...

2.4 Sexual Health

In small groups discuss what the term 'sexual health' means. Once you have decided on your definition write it in the space provided. Then write down four questions you would like to ask to extend your knowledge and understanding of sexual health. Finally, write down what assumptions you might make about someone who is in good sexual health.

Sexual health means …

Four questions we would ask:

1

2

3

4

Being in good sexual health would mean …

PLTS in PSHE: Creative Thinkers

© Folens (copiable page)

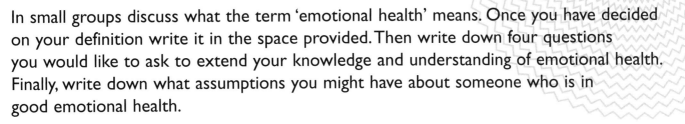

2.5 Emotional Health

In small groups discuss what the term 'emotional health' means. Once you have decided on your definition write it in the space provided. Then write down four questions you would like to ask to extend your knowledge and understanding of emotional health. Finally, write down what assumptions you might have about someone who is in good emotional health.

Emotional health means …

Four questions we would ask:

1

2

3

4

Being in good emotional health would mean …

2.6 What Does It Mean?

You will need Activity sheets 2.1–2.5 to use with this sheet.

Working in the same small group as before, read through your definitions of the various aspects of health. What have you assumed about individuals and their good/bad health? Write these assumptions down in the first box.

Your task is to come up with ideas to make young people aged 11–14 more aware of the different areas of their health and to suggest new initiatives or new alternatives to existing initiatives to 'make our young people more healthy'. Write your ideas in the second box.

Our assumptions:

Our ideas/new solutions:

PLTS in PSHE: Creative Thinkers   © Folens (copiable page)

Teacher's Notes

Objectives

By the end of the lesson, students will:

◎ understand the different roles and responsibilities young people have.

◎ have examined the feelings and emotions aroused by those roles and responsibilities.

◎ be able to ask questions to extend their thinking.

◎ be able to generate ideas and explore possibilities.

Prior knowledge

None.

Links

Personal, Social, Health and Economic Education Programmes of Study for England: Personal Wellbeing: 1.1 Personal identities; 1.3 Risk; 1.4 Relationships.

Curriculum for Excellence for Scotland: Health and Wellbeing: Mental, emotional, social and physical wellbeing; Relationships, sexual health and parenthood.

Personal and Social Education Framework for Wales: Health and emotional wellbeing.

Revised Curriculum for Northern Ireland: Learning for Life and Work: Personal development.

Background

All individuals enter into a wide range of relationships. All relationships carry with them roles, responsibilities and risks. Students need to be able to look at the relationships they have and understand the concept of responsibility within those relationships.

Starter activity

Examine the meaning of the words 'roles' and 'responsibilities' and decide on definitions. Suggested definitions are: 'role' – what a person is expected to do/fulfil; responsibilities – actions for which a person is morally accountable.

Activity sheets

Activity sheet **3.1 Roles And Responsibilities** should be worked on in groups of three. Students should discuss what roles young people of their age have and then go on to examine the responsibilities they have. From this they should examine the barriers that might prevent them from taking other roles in society. Finally they are asked to think about what other roles young people could have. If they find this difficult to think about give them some hints, e.g. young people can be parents, carers, workers, mentors, etc. Activity sheet **3.2 Feelings And Emotions** can be brought in here. It takes the concept of roles and responsibilities further, asking students to examine the feelings and emotions they have experienced.

Activity sheet **3.3 Risks In Relationships** should be completed in small groups. Students should talk in their groups about times when they took risks in relationships – any kind of relationships – and what happened. This is a very sensitive area and must be treated with respect and empathy by all.

Activity sheet **3.4 Skills You Need** is based on what a group of Year 9 students said about relationships and linked skills. Students are asked to discuss the skills listed and to say whether or not they agree with them. They are also asked to add other skills to the list.

Plenary

Look at what makes a good relationship and link the views on that to what has been learned in this unit.

3.1 Roles And Responsibilities

You should work in small groups for this activity. Below are a number of questions for you to answer. Discuss each question and then write your group answer in the space provided.

a What roles do young people of your age have?

b What responsibilities do young people of your age have?

c What stops young people from having other roles in society?

d What other roles do you think it could be possible for young people to have?

PLTS in PSHE: Creative Thinkers
© Folens (copiable page)

3.2 Feelings And Emotions

You will need Activity sheet 3.1 to use with this sheet.

On sheet 3.1 you looked at the roles and responsibilities young people have – and those they could have if allowed to do so. This sheet takes the concepts of feelings and emotions and links them to roles and responsibilities. Write down two roles and two responsibilities you identified on sheet 3.1 and for each one say what emotions and feelings they might create. One example has been completed for you.

Role/Responsibility	Emotions/Feelings
Grandchild	Love; worry; concern; anger when people laugh at my gran because she forgets things; worried about growing old.

3.3 Risks In Relationships

Everyone takes risks in relationships. Some risks are for good reasons – others for bad! In your groups, share occasions when you took risks in relationships. Talk about what risks you took and how things worked out. Talk about the pressures you were under when you took those risks.

After listening to what everyone in the group has to say you should complete this activity sheet on your own.

How were the various risks taken by those in the group the same?

How were they different?

Choose one risk that someone described and write down two questions you would ask them to help you understand more about their risk.

1

2

Why do you think there are so many similarities in people's experiences?

How do you think risk taking in relationships will change as you grow up?

PLTS in PSHE: Creative Thinkers

3.4 Skills You Need

This sheet is based on what 200 Year 9 students suggested were important skills in relationships. Read through the skills below and discuss them in small groups. Do you agree or disagree with any of them? Add two other skills in the empty boxes.

To listen

To keep quiet if necessary

To be sympathetic

To close your ears to criticism

To be able to laugh with them

To be able to say 'sorry' and mean it

To be able to cry with them

Not to show you are bored even when you are

To tell little lies if necessary

To be able to read thoughts and minds

To give a hug and not be embarrassed

To accept that you are not always right

Teacher's Notes

Objectives

By the end of the lesson, students will:

◎ understand the different attitudes young people have towards money and savings.

◎ understand the concept of risk taking and enterprise.

◎ be able to ask questions to extend their thinking.

◎ be able to connect their own and others' experiences in inventive ways.

Prior knowledge

None.

Links

Personal, Social, Health and Economic Education Programmes of Study for England: Personal Wellbeing: 1.1 Personal identities; 1.3 Risk. Economic wellbeing and financial capability: 1.2 Capability; 1.3 Risk; 1.4 Economic understanding.

Curriculum for Excellence for Scotland: Health and Wellbeing: Health and Wellbeing: Mental, emotional, social and physical wellbeing.

Personal and Social Education Framework for Wales: Active citizenship.

Revised Curriculum for Northern Ireland: Learning for Life and Work: Employability.

Background

All students are required to learn how to be enterprising. They are also required to understand the concept of financial capability and to develop a 'can-do' approach to problem solving. Within all this students learn to challenge assumptions, set targets and manage money. In the twenty-first century these skills and attributes are at the forefront of much educational thinking and students are encouraged to be confident and responsible citizens who can make a positive contribution to their local, national and international communities.

Starter activity

Use real examples of money to look at the symbols and emblems used. What do they mean? Why have those symbols and emblems in particular been used? Why is money so important to us that we have very sophisticated coins and notes?

Activity sheets

Activity sheet **4.1 My Money** asks students to examine their own money: how much they receive, how they spend it and to compare their results with others in the class. In looking at other ways they could make money, stress that it must be legal! In looking at how they could use their money to help others the obvious answer would be to give to charity but there are other ways, e.g. to sponsor a child in a less economically developed country; to sponsor an animal; to buy a small gift each week for someone who needs a friend.

Activity sheet **4.2 Risks And Rewards** and Activity sheets **4.3 The Activity (1)** and **4.4 The Activity (2)** ask students to plan an activity for Year 7 students and then carry the activity out – with the aim of making a profit on their initial £50. This whole activity could be done as part of a planned day for students and the best activity could be carried out at the end of the day. This could in turn lead to a termly or yearly event based on these activities.

Activity sheet **4.5 Life Without Money** asks students to imagine a country where no money is used. The aim of this sheet is to give students an insight into how dependent modern society is on money and to look at alternatives, e.g. bartering. As students work on this activity you should add extra ideas in at various points, e.g. the government could decide that people could be used as currency – who would then be most valuable and why?

Plenary

Should the world have one currency? What would be the advantages/disadvantages of this idea?

4.1 My Money

Answer the questions below:

How much money do you receive every week and how do you use it?
Do you think you use it wisely? Give reasons.
How do others use their money? Talk to three other students in your class and write their answers down.
What new ways could you find to gain more money? Talk to others in the class and come up with some different ideas.
What other possible ways are there for you to use your money? Could you use some of it to help others? How?

4.2 Risks And Rewards

A team of Year 8 students took part in a challenge. Their task was to decide on one or more activities which would allow them to make a profit from the £50 they had been given.

The activity had to be:

◎ aimed at Year 7 students
◎ done in school – but could take place before or after school
◎ open to all levels of ability.

They had to:

◎ work in teams of six
◎ generate ideas and explore possibilities
◎ connect their own ideas and experiences to the task planned
◎ be inventive – more marks were given for this
◎ question what was planned if they had problems with it
◎ suggest alternatives to anything they did not like
◎ follow the activity through from start to finish
◎ adapt their idea/activity as needed
◎ make a profit!

4.3 The Activity (1)

Your task is to plan an activity for Year 7 students and carry it out. Look at Activity sheet 4.2 for the rules you have to follow.

Activity sheets 4.3 and 4.4 are your planning sheets. Working as a team you should complete the boxes with the required information.

Write down the names of the people in your team. Beside each name write down the two special skills/attributes they bring to the team:

1

2

3

4

5

6

Our activity will be:

This is a brief description of it:

4.4 The Activity (2)

We came up with these initial ideas:

Our own experiences in Year 7 helped us because:

Issues we discussed when deciding on the activity were:

If circumstances changed we could adapt the activity by:

PLTS in PSHE: Creative Thinkers

4.5 Life Without Money

Imagine a country where no one used money at all. How could you get what you needed and wanted? Your task is to work in a small group and decide how a country would be run without money and how individuals in that country would be able to manage.

Your country is called Zarubia. It is an island about the size of England and has 30 million inhabitants. The government has decided to encourage other methods rather than using money. You need to think about:

◎   How could people be paid?
◎   How could people 'buy' things?
◎   How could the government run the country without taxes?
◎   How could the government provide services, e.g. schools, hospitals, etc.

When you have decided on your ideas you must present them to the class.

Imagine a life without money!

> **Remember:**
>
> ◎   be creative and imaginative
>
> ◎   explore possibilities
>
> ◎   make original connections
>
> ◎   think of different ways to come up with solutions
>
> ◎   work with the others in your group
>
> ◎   make sure your ideas are workable and valuable.

Objectives

By the end of the lesson, students will:

◎ understand the concepts of long and short term planning.

◎ understand the concept of risk taking and enterprise.

◎ understand the need to adapt ideas as circumstances change.

◎ be able to try out alternatives or new solutions and follow ideas through.

Prior knowledge

None.

Links

Personal, Social, Health and Economic Education Programmes of Study for England: Personal Wellbeing: 1.1 Personal identities; 1.3 Risk; 1.5 Diversity. Economic wellbeing and financial capability: 1.3 Risk; 1.4 Economic understanding.

Curriculum for Excellence for Scotland: Health and Wellbeing: Mental, emotional, social and physical wellbeing.

Personal and Social Education Framework for Wales: Health and emotional wellbeing; Active citizenship; Sustainable development and global citizenship.

Revised Curriculum for Northern Ireland: Learning for Life and Work: Personal development; Local and global citizenship.

Background

Students are often confronted by images of disasters and by appeals for help in both financial and physical terms. Global responsibility and active/global citizenship are an accepted part of education and of society. The many charity appeals on TV and radio have served to make young people aware of disasters and their effects on people and lives. Responding to a disaster requires large-scale planning as well as an understanding of the people and cultures in the disaster area.

Starter activity

Use images from a recent disaster appeal to examine what is being asked for, how and why.

Activity sheets

Activity sheet **5.1 It Happened Like This …** sets the scene for the unit and all the activities within it. Read this sheet as a class and discuss what it says. Look at what an earthquake can do and the destruction it can cause. Some images from the internet would help with this.

Activity sheet **5.2 The Cost Of Help** gives basic costs for various items needed for the disaster recovery programme. You could make up other costs for students to work with. The total sum of money available is £10 million; you could, at times during the activities, add to this by telling students about extra donations.

Activity sheets **5.3 Start Planning – Short Term** and **5.4 Start Planning – Long Term** ask students to decide on the top ten short term and long term priorities for the island and encourage them to discuss in groups what is most needed and why. Students should be encouraged to think creatively and find imaginative ways to deal with the problems on the island.

Activity sheet **5.5 Preventing It Happening Again** asks students to plan for the future of the island and to look at ideas so that the island will be more prepared for possible future disasters. At the end of this task the teacher should mark each team's efforts – the areas to be marked are shown on the Activity sheet. A prize could be given to the group who have come up with the best ideas.

Plenary

Watch a short film or video from a charity about their work in a disaster area. What did they do for short and long term help? Was it the same as or different to what the students planned? This will obviously depend on what is happening in the world at the time you are teaching this topic, but suggested websites are www.christianaid.org.uk; www.oxfam.org.uk; www.redcross.org.uk.

Tears in paradise

An eyewitness report from the scene of the earthquake by Danni Robins

At 3.32am yesterday, on this beautiful island, an earthquake struck which left thousands dead and thousands more homeless. No buildings have been left standing and we are being forced to find what shelter we can. Many holidaymakers and islanders are injured and the only hospital here lies in ruins. The dead have been left where they died and everyone here is still in total shock. We need help, any kind of help if we are to survive. Already people are becoming ill from the effects of blood loss, dirty water and no shelter.

We were all in our beds when it happened and there was no warning at all. Suddenly the hotel I was staying in rocked and I was thrown from my bed. As I looked out of my window I saw deep chasms opening up in the roads and fields. Whole houses and hotels disappeared down these gigantic holes. The whole thing was totally terrifying. Like many others I have only the clothes I am wearing and I am scavenging for food among the ruins of the hotels and houses. I fear that looting might start – although there isn't much left to loot. Come on world – we need help now! This will be my one and only text report – help us!

5.2 The Cost Of Help

Use this sheet to help you with the work on Activity sheets 5.3 and 5.4.

You are a member of the emergency planning team which has been given the task of providing short and long term help to the island. You have a 'pot' of £10 million for this.

Things you should know:

- There are 30,000 islanders living on the island.
- There are estimated to be 10,000 visitors on the island.
- You have no idea how many people are still alive.
- A basic home will cost £500 to build.
- A tent will cost £50 to put up and equip.
- Medical equipment and the tent required for a field hospital will cost £50,000.
- Food will cost £15 a week for each person.
- Clothing will cost £20 for each person.
- The volunteers going out to help need no wages but you will need to hire vans/cars/helicopters and pay for fuel for them.
- You will need to find and bury the dead and this will have to be paid for.
- You will need to search for anyone trapped in buildings etc. and this will have to be paid for.

PLTS in PSHE: Creative Thinkers

5.3 Start Planning – Short Term

You will need Activity sheets 5.1 and 5.2 to help you with this activity.

Your team's task is to plan what needs to be done in the *short term* to help the people on the island. Your team must decide on the top ten *short term* priorities and price them. You must think in a creative way, exploring all ideas, thinking of different ways to tackle the problem and working as a team to find imaginative solutions and outcomes. List your team's top ten priorities in the table below and for each one say why you have chosen it.

	Priority	Reason
1		
2		
3		
4		
5		
6		
7		
8		
9		
10		

5.4 Start Planning – Long Term

You will need Activity sheets 5.1–5.3 to help you with this activity.

Your team's task is to plan what needs to be done in the *long term* to help the people on the island. Your team must decide on the top ten *long term* priorities and price them. You must think in a creative way, exploring all ideas, thinking of different ways to tackle the problem and working as a team to find imaginative solutions and outcomes. List your team's top ten priorities in the table below and for each one say why you have chosen it.

	Priority	Reason
1		
2		
3		
4		
5		
6		
7		
8		
9		
10		

PLTS in PSHE: Creative Thinkers

5.5 Preventing It Happening Again

It is not yet possible to stop an earthquake from happening. However, there might be ways of minimising the effects of an earthquake and of warning people when one is about to happen. Your task is to make plans for the island so that:

a the people on the island are warned if an earthquake is forecast
b the buildings are 'earthquake ready'
c emergency plans are ready to put into operation at short notice.

You are working in the same emergency planning teams. The problem facing your team is laid out for you above. How will you solve it? Your teacher will mark you as a team for:

◎ generating ideas
◎ coming up with questions to help extend your thinking and planning
◎ connecting everyone's ideas and experiences in inventive and different ways
◎ asking questions about assumptions
◎ suggesting new and different solutions
◎ suggesting adaptations to ideas if circumstances change.

Objectives

By the end of the lesson, students will:

◎ understand the risks young people place themselves in with regards to sex.
◎ understand the concept of actions having consequences.
◎ be able to try out alternatives or new solutions and follow ideas through.
◎ understand the need to adapt ideas as circumstances change.

Prior knowledge

None.

Links

Personal, Social, Health and Economic Education Programmes of Study for England: Personal Wellbeing: 1.1 Personal identities; 1.2 Healthy lifestyles; 1.3 Risk; 1.4 Relationships.

Curriculum for Excellence for Scotland: Health and Wellbeing: Mental, emotional, social and physical wellbeing; Relationships, sexual health and parenthood.

Personal and Social Education Framework for Wales: Health and emotional wellbeing; Moral and spiritual development.

Revised Curriculum for Northern Ireland: Learning for Life and Work: Personal development.

Background

Britain has the highest level of teenage pregnancy in Western Europe. The government's Teenage Pregnancy Strategy aims to halve the number of teenage pregnancies by 2010 – starting from a 1998 baseline. Every day 21 girls under the age of 16 become pregnant in Britain. Figures for 2006 show that 39,000 under-18s became pregnant in that year, which equates to 42 in every 1000. Of those, 49 per cent had legal abortions. For 13–15 year olds the figure was 7.7 in every 1000 with 60 per cent having legal abortions. The teenage pregnancy figures for 2006 were the lowest for over 20 years but the 50 per cent reduction by 2010 seems unlikely to be reached. The latest figures (available in February 2009) show that in England and Wales there has been an increase in the pregnancy rates among 15–17 year olds. The figure has gone up from 40.9 per 1000 to 41.9 per 1000. This is the first increase since 2002. (Figures from www.everychildmatters.gov.uk.)

Starter activity

Discuss what the best age to have a child is, and why.

Activity sheets

Activity sheet **6.1 When Tom Met Danni** introduces a 'typical' couple who have a one night stand. According to recent statistics one third of 16–25 year olds have sex under the influence of alcohol and this is reflected in the events recorded on the sheet.

Activity sheet **6.2 Consequences (1)** asks students to work in pairs and highlight points in the story where choices had to be made. Students should then consider what would have happened if different choices had been made – with the choices being up to the students.

Activity sheet **6.3 Consequences (2)** takes the story a step further with Danni's announcement of her pregnancy. Students look at the choices available to the couple and at what they could do. The activity is then brought to a conclusion by saying what the outcome of each choice might be.

Activity Sheet **6.4 Twenty Years On ...** should be used with Activity sheets **6.2** and **6.3**. Students follow through two of their ideas to look at what the situation might be like 20 years later. Students should be encouraged to think 'outside the box' for this activity. For example what if Tom and Danni had decided to have the baby adopted and 20 years later wondered what she/he was like and tried to find out?

Activity sheet **6.5 Rewind** takes students back to the original story – they will need Activity sheet 6.1 – and asks them to rewrite the story, looking at different possibilities and outcomes. Encourage students to use their own experiences and ideas here. Read out the following changes at various points during the story of 'When Tom met Danni' and ask students to change their story to suit the changes given.

1. Jack couldn't go home during the day.
2. Danni hadn't been drinking.
3. Tom didn't fancy Danni.
4. The garden shed was locked!

Plenary

Discuss with students why teenagers get pregnant when contraception is readily available.

Tom and Danni are both sixteen. This is the story of how and when they met …
Jack's parents had gone away on holiday and Jack had to stay with his grandparents.
His parents said he could go home during the day but had to sleep at his
grandparents 'to avoid any problems'. Jack asked about twenty friends to go
round to his house at 10:00am for a 'day binge'. Around 60 people turned up
'and it was mint'.

Danni didn't know Jack but a friend of a friend invited her and because it was
boring sitting at home in the holidays she went along. Tom didn't know Jack either
but he knew Jack's best friend, Zig.

Tom was in the garden lying down on the lawn when Danni walked out through the
patio doors. Tom thought she looked fit and shouted for her to come over. Danni
thought Tom was OK and went over to him. She was a bit bored by then because
the party was loud and stupid and most people were drinking and being sick. She
didn't mind the drinking, she had drunk quite a bit herself, but she hated the being
sick.

Before she knew it Tom was kissing her all over her face and neck – he stank of
booze. A couple came out of the garden shed and Tom said, 'Let's go in there – it's
quiet and cosy'. So Danni followed Tom and 30 minutes later when they came out of
the shed she wasn't a virgin anymore.

Tom asked her out and she agreed to meet him the next evening. They went bowling
and she won. She didn't really think much of him and told him she didn't want to
see him again.

6.2 Consequences (1)

You will need Activity sheet 6.1 for this activity.

Working in pairs, read through the story of when Tom and Danni met and use a highlighter pen to mark any text where Tom or Danni made a choice. Then for each of those highlighted choices write down what might have happened if different choices had been made.

Make sure you discuss all the options, even those that are not that obvious.

Use the space below to write on. If you need extra space you can use the other side of this sheet.

_____

_____

_____

_____

_____

_____

_____

_____

_____

_____

_____

_____

PLTS in PSHE: Creative Thinkers © Folens (copiable page)

6.3 Consequences (2)

You will need Activity sheet 6.1 for this activity.

Six weeks after Tom met Danni he received a phone call. It wasn't good news. Danni was calling to say that she was pregnant and that he, Tom, was the father. She hadn't told anyone else and wanted to meet with him to talk about what they should do.
What could/should they do?

Your task is to work in pairs to explore ideas about what could/should happen.
Try to think about all the options, not just the most obvious – but in every case
you must be able to follow the idea through to the end, i.e. say what will happen at
each step of the way and what you think will the final outcome for each of your ideas.
Write your ideas in the table below. If you need more space use the other side of this sheet.

What could/should happen?	What will happen next?	What will happen after that?	Final outcome

6.4 Twenty Years On ...

Take one of the alternative ideas you decided on for Activity sheet 6.3 and work it through as follows:

It is 20 years later. Tom and Danni are both 36. They discuss what happened (i.e. your alternative idea), and they look at how their lives have developed and what would have happened if they had made different choices (i.e. another of your alternative ideas!).

Your task, working in pairs, is to:

a Decide what happened after they chose your first alternative idea and write it down.

b Decide what could have happened if they had chosen your second alternative idea and write it down.

Idea 1:

Idea 2:

PLTS in PSHE: Creative Thinkers

© Folens (copiable page)

6.5 Rewind

You will need Activity sheet 6.1 for this activity.

As you have already seen, the story of Tom and Danni could have been very different. Your task is to work in pairs and discuss the original story, looking at different possibilities and adapting ideas as circumstances change (and they will because your teacher will tell you some changes at various points as you are working).

Once you have discussed the new version of the story you should rewrite it using your ideas and experiences to make the story different and believable.

Use the space below for your initial ideas and then rewrite your story using another sheet of paper.

When Tom met Danni (Take 2):

_____

_____

_____

_____

_____

_____

_____

_____

_____

_____

_____

Teacher's Notes

Objectives

By the end of the lesson, students will:

◎ understand the different types of relationships young people can be involved in.

◎ understand attitudes to homosexuality.

◎ be able to connect their own and others' assumptions.

◎ understand the need to adapt ideas as circumstances change.

Prior knowledge

Students know that the age for sexual consent is 16 – for both heterosexual and homosexual sex.

Links

Personal, Social, Health and Economic Education Programmes of Study for England: Personal Wellbeing: 1.1 Personal identities; 1.2 Healthy lifestyles; 1.3 Risk; 1.4 Relationships; 1.5 Diversity.

Curriculum for Excellence for Scotland: Health and Wellbeing: Health and Wellbeing: Mental, emotional, social and physical wellbeing; Relationships, sexual health and parenthood.

Personal and Social Education Framework for Wales: Health and emotional wellbeing; Moral and spiritual development.

Revised Curriculum for Northern Ireland: Learning for Life and Work: Personal development.

Background

For many young people the biggest concerns and worries they have are linked to relationships. These are relationships with family, with friends and with boyfriends and girlfriends.

A large number of young people feel that parents/carers do not understand them or their lives and at times family relationships can break down, causing major concerns and problems for all involved. For some young people the *framily*, i.e. friends who act as family, are as important as – and at times more important than – 'real' family. For some cultures, as with some individuals, the acceptance of homosexuality is difficult and can lead to divisions in the family.

Starter activity

Ask students to write down the names of their best friends and for each one say why they are best friends.

Activity sheets

Activity sheet **7.1 Introducing The Six Friends** should be used together with Activity sheet **7.2 Understanding Relationships**. Students are asked to look at the 'problem' of Raj admitting to his sexuality and the consequences of that admission. Within the activity they are asked to look at their own attitudes and assumptions towards homosexuals. This could prove difficult for some young people and should be treated with care and consideration. Many young men find it difficult to discuss homosexuality. Discuss with them why Raj went out with Chloe in Year 9. Also discuss why they think Raj has 'come out' at this particular time.

Activity sheet **7.3 The Pressures We Face** looks at the different kinds of pressures young people face in their relationships and should be used with Activity sheets **7.1 Introducing The Six Friends** and **7.4 The Challenges Of Relationships**. Working in pairs students should examine the problems and pressures each of the friends face and decide on solutions for them to ease their relationship problems. There are no right or wrong answers here and students should be given the chance to put forward their views in an open forum.

Activity sheet **7.5 My Relationships** links what students have looked at with the six friends to their own relationships and encourages them to examine the pressures they have in their own relationships. This work is very personal and should be done individually with no one being forced to give their opinions.

Plenary

Look at a couple or family in the news at the moment and examine what pressures they face and decide on ways in which the pressures could be relieved.

7.1 Introducing The Six Friends

These six young people met in Year 7 and have been firm friends ever since. They are now in Year 11. All are 16 and they are just weeks away from leaving school.

Jaz

Marnie

Chloe

Andy

Raj

Ash

7.2 Understanding Relationships

You will need Activity sheet 7.1 for this activity.

Raj has just told Chloe that he is gay and he wants her advice about how to tell the rest of their friends and his family. He says that his family will be very unhappy about his sexuality. Chloe is very surprised and tells Raj, 'I never for one minute thought you would be gay. Now if Ash had told me he was gay – that I would understand'. In pairs, work through the following questions:

a   Think about how Raj should tell his family about his sexuality. When would be the best time for this? What should he say? Who should he tell first – or should he tell his family all together?

b   Think about how Raj should tell his four close friends. Should he tell them together or one at a time?

c   Think about your own assumptions about someone who is gay. How would you react to a friend telling you that he or she was homosexual?

d   Follow your ideas through and look at possible reactions and repercussions for Raj when he 'comes out' to his family and friends.

e   Discuss why Raj told Chloe first. Chloe and Raj went out together in Year 9 for a while!

PLTS in PSHE: Creative Thinkers

7.3 The Pressures We Face

All relationships present pressures. Read what the six friends say about the pressures in their relationships.

You get pressure from boys who expect you to do what they want; parents who push you too hard; friends who want your time.

Jaz

The colour of my skin causes me pressure, especially when I go out with my boyfriend, Andy. I also get pressure from my family who want me to do things that they couldn't.

Marnie

Pressure when friends confide in you, like Raj; pressure from mum and dad about the time I come home; pressure from Jaz who is a real brainbox!

Chloe

I get pressure from Marnie about the fact that she is black and I am white; and pressure from Ash to party all the time.

Andy

I feel pressure from my gay friends to 'come out'; and the build up of pressure about what will happen when I do.

Raj

Pressure from family and friends to 'work hard' when all I want to do is enjoy myself; pressure from other kids in school who say I look like a girl.

Ash

7.4 The Challenges Of Relationships

You will need Activity sheets 7.1 and 7.3 for this activity.

Work in pairs. For each of the six friends you must look at ways in which they can tackle the problems and pressures they face in relationships and come up with solutions for them to make their relationships easier.

Before you start you must make sure you explore what the real problems and pressures are and perhaps use your own experiences to help sort out their problems. Use the spaces given below to write down your answers to their pressures and problems.

Jaz:

Marnie:

Chloe:

Andy:

Raj:

Ash:

7.5 My Relationships

Think about your relationships with family and friends. What are the pressures your relationships put you under? Are there any ways you could sort out or lessen those pressures?

In the table below, write down the six biggest pressures you face in your different relationships and then, for each one, write down ideas for sorting out those pressures and problems.

NOTE: This work should be done privately without any discussion with anyone else.

1
2
3
4
5
6

Objectives

By the end of the lesson, students will:

◎ understand the different stages needed in large scale planning.

◎ understand how to develop an argument to persuade and convince.

◎ understand how to connect their own and others' experiences in inventive ways.

◎ understand how important it is to be able to adapt ideas as circumstances change.

Prior knowledge

If they do not already know you will need to explain what a 'prom' is – see below in 'Background'.

Links

Personal, Social, Health and Economic Education Programmes of Study for England: Personal Wellbeing: 1.1 Personal identities; 1.3 Risk. Economic wellbeing and financial capability: 1.2 Capability.

Curriculum for Excellence for Scotland: Health and Wellbeing: Health and Wellbeing: Mental, emotional, social and physical wellbeing.

Personal and Social Education Framework for Wales: Health and emotional wellbeing; Active citizenship; Moral and spiritual development.

Revised Curriculum for Northern Ireland: Learning for Life and Work: Personal development; Local and global citizenship.

Background

The prom – or 'promenade' – originated in the USA and is now a part of life for many schools in the UK. A prom is usually held at the end of Year 11 and/or 13 and requires formal wear, a booked venue with food and major expense for parents/carers. Proms are now big business in the UK and have even extended down to some nursery schools where they have proms for those leaving nursery to start school. Venues are often booked a full year ahead and 'prom fever' can grip a whole year group. Some schools are rejecting the whole prom concept and looking to change the idea to one which is more school-based and less expensive.

Starter activity

Show the class some images from the Internet showing UK proms and discuss what they show

Activity sheets

Activity sheet **8.1 The Decision!** sets the scene for the unit. It should be used with Activity sheet **8.2 Reasons And Ideas**. Students are asked to work out the main reasons why the prom has been cancelled at Hall View School and for each one they should consider how the problem could be resolved. Some of the reasons are made very clear while others are alluded to.

Activity sheet **8.3 The Solution** asks students to outline the main aspects of their 'alternative' prom with adaptations which could be put in place if necessary. Within this context students are expected to come up with different ideas based on what the headteacher says in her letter and what they think Year 11 students would like and want.

Activity sheets **8.4 The Big Sell (1)** and **8.5 The Big Sell (2)** should be used together. Students should use Activity sheet **8.4** to work out their ideas for convincing the students that their alternative prom will be just what they want, and to map out their ideas for the advert/flyer. On Activity sheet **8.5** they should create the advert. Students may wish to do this using ICT instead of on paper. This activity could be extended to look in more detail at the kind of clothing to be worn, food for the occasion, music and decorations.

Plenary

Should nursery children have proms? What do students think about this concept?

HALL VIEW SCHOOL

Dear Year 11 students

An 'alternative prom'!

After a great deal of thought and many meetings it has been decided that the current practice of having a prom outside school will be discontinued. The prom last year was beset with many problems and the staff felt that we needed a total rethink on it. We feel that the amount of money spent on the prom by individual students is now out of control and has led to many students not attending. Added to this is the problem that some students are consuming alcohol at the prom, which is absolutely not allowed. It is the general consensus among the staff that we need to reappraise the prom and consider what we do and why we do it.

I am therefore challenging you all to think creatively about the 'alternative prom' and to explore ideas for it. Come up with original ideas, think about different ways of celebrating your five years with us at Hall View. All your ideas will be looked at and we will allow you, the students, to decide which of the ideas we shortlist you would like to attend. Once the decision has been made we will set up a team of Year 11 students to plan and organise the 'alternative prom'.

Put your thinking caps on and come up with some exciting and innovative ideas but remember: the 'alternative prom' must take place in school and costs must be minimal i.e. no more than £20 per student for a ticket. I look forward to hearing your suggestions

Yours sincerely

Mrs Glaser

Headteacher

8.2 Reasons And Ideas

a Look at Activity sheet 8.1. What are the reasons for the established prom being cancelled? Some of the reasons are obvious, others are not. Your first task is to read behind what is written and decide on the main five reasons. Write them down in the table below. You should work in small groups of three or four for this activity.

Reasons for the cancellation:
1
2
3
4
5

b Now take each of the five reasons and think about what could be done to sort out the problem. Write your answers in the table below.

What could be done?
1
2
3
4
5

PLTS in PSHE: Creative Thinkers   © Folens (copiable page)

8.3 The Solution

Now it's time to decide on the plan for your 'alternative prom'. You must convince Mrs Glaser, the headteacher, that your idea is the one to choose.

On this page you should write down what form the prom should take, and outline the six main points to your plan in order to convince her and the rest of the staff that your idea is the best – and that they will be acceptable not only to this year's Year 11 students but to students in the future. You must also show that your ideas could be adapted if circumstances were to change at any time.

Use the table below to outline your ideas. You should work in small groups of three or four for this activity.

The 'alternative prom' will be:
1
2
3
4
5
6
7
8
9

8.4 The Big Sell (1)

Mrs Glaser likes your idea and so does the rest of the staff. Now you have an even more difficult task – to convince the Year 11 students that this will be great!

First decide on a name for the event and then jot down notes for an advert or flyer which you will give out to every Year 11 student to convince them to attend. You should work in small groups of three or four for this activity.

The name for the event is:

_____

Our ideas for our advert are:

_____

_____

_____

_____

_____

_____

_____

_____

_____

_____

8.5 The Big Sell (2)

You will need Activity sheet 8.4 for this activity. Use the ideas you discussed to create the advert for your 'alternative prom.' Your advert must appeal to Year 11 students.

Teacher's Notes

Objectives

By the end of the lesson, students will:

◎ understand the meaning of being 'in debt' and the effects that can have on a family.

◎ understand the difference between what is necessary to live and what is meant by 'extras'.

◎ understand how to generate ideas and explore different possibilities.

◎ be able to question their own and others' assumptions.

Prior knowledge

None.

Links

Personal, Social, Health and Economic Education Programmes of Study for England: Personal Wellbeing: 1.1 Personal identities; 1.2 Healthy lifestyles; 1.3 Risk; 1.4 Relationships. Economic wellbeing and financial capability: 1.2 Capability; 1.3 Risk; 1.4 Economic understanding.

Curriculum for Excellence for Scotland: Health and Wellbeing: Health and Wellbeing: Mental, emotional, social and physical wellbeing.

Personal and Social Education Framework for Wales: Health and emotional wellbeing; Active citizenship; Moral and spiritual development.

Revised Curriculum for Northern Ireland: Learning for Life and Work: Personal development; Local and global citizenship; Employability.

Background

In the current (February 2009) financial climate more and more people are in debt. Some Citizens Advice Bureaus (CAB) say that in just three months they have seen a 30 per cent rise in those seeking help with debt problems. Rising prices for food and fuel are said to have put many families into debt with mortgages and loans being the biggest problems. Since October 2007 CAB have advised 77,000 new callers worried about debt. Over half of the callers were aged 35–49. However a recent CAB study in Scotland shows that some over-60s (Scotland only) have debt levels of 29 times their monthly income. CAB says that the debt problem is set to worsen as Britain goes further into recession.

Starter activity

Look at the reasons why people get into debt and discuss what students understand by being 'in debt.'

Activity sheets

Activity sheet 9.**1 Money In/Money Out** shows the monthly income/expenditure of Molly and Sean and should be used alongside Activity sheet **8.2 In Debt** to discuss what is happening and why it has happened. Students could extend the discussion by looking at the effects the situation is having on the two children as well as on Molly and Sean. Students could also look at why Sean does not want Molly to ask her parents for help and why Sean hides letters.

Activity sheet **9.3 Possible Solutions – Short Term** should be used with the previous two Activity sheets to look at what possible solutions there could be, in the short term, to Molly and Sean's problems while examining the effects those solutions could have on the family and on individuals in the family.

Activity sheet **9.4 Possible Solutions – Long Term** should be used with the Activity sheets **9.1–9.3** to examine the longer term changes Molly and Sean need to make in order to break the cycle of debt. Students also have to look at the effects these changes will have on the lives of the family. You could extend this work by looking at the 'what if …' scenario, i.e. if they don't sort out their money problems what might happen short/long term to the family and to each of them as individuals.

Plenary

Go to the Citizens Advice Bureau website – www.citizensadvice.org.uk – and look at the 'Press Office' section – it contains facts, reports, etc. on debt. Discuss this information with students.

PLTS in PSHE: Creative Thinkers

9.1 Money In/Money Out

Sean and Molly work hard. Their two children enjoy lots of holidays and treats. The family lives in a comfortable home and in the words of Molly's mum, 'they want for nothing'. Their monthly income and expenditure look like this:

Money in every month:

- Sean's salary: £1,700

- Molly's salary: £800

- Child Benefit: £132.80

- Total money in is: **£2,632.80**

They have no savings.

Money out every month:

- Mortgage: £1,200

- Council tax: £130

- Utilities – water, gas, electricity: £140

- Food: £400

- Credit card payments: £280

- Car credit: £90

- Car tax and insurance for two cars: £65

- TV licence: £12

- House and personal insurance: £60

- Going out: £250

- Clothes: £200

- Childminder/after school clubs: £40

- Hairdresser/gym: £80

- Ballet/judo classes for children: £80

- Cigarettes: £120

- Total money out is: **£2,897**

9.2 In Debt

Sean and Molly are in debt. That means they cannot pay all their bills – they do not earn enough money to cover all the money they are paying out. For the past six months they have been using their credit cards to give them extra money every month but now they are aware that they are in trouble and need to sort something out.

Their health is suffering because of the worry. Molly cannot sleep at night and she and Sean fight all the time. This is affecting their two daughters who have started to misbehave at school and at home. Molly wants to ask her parents to loan them some money to pay off some of their bills but Sean does not want his in-laws to know that they are in debt.

They are receiving letters about their debt and Sean has started to hide the letters from Molly. People often phone them about their debt and they don't know what to do next. They are worried that they will not be able to pay their mortgage and so will lose their home and have nowhere to live.

Molly cannot concentrate on her work at a call centre. Sean's boss knows something is wrong but doesn't like to ask him about it. They are trying to keep going and do all the things they usually do but it is very hard for them. After many weeks of worry Molly cannot eat or sleep and looks terrible. Her mum tells her to go to the doctor because she is worried that there must be something very wrong.

PLTS in PSHE: Creative Thinkers

9.3 Possible Solutions – Short Term

You will need Activity sheets 9.1 and 9.2 for this activity.

What could Sean and Molly do to improve their situation? Working in pairs, look at how much money comes in and how much goes out each month and discuss what the couple could change. List the changes and assess how they might help and how much money would be saved in the table below. See if you can tip the balance so that Molly and Sean earn more money than they spend.

Changes	How would this help?	££ saved

9.4 Possible Solutions – Long Term

You will need Activity sheets 9.1–9.3 for this activity.

What could Sean and Molly do to improve their situation in the long term? Work in pairs and look at how they could make big changes to make sure they do not get into debt again. One possible solution has been done for you. For each solution say how it will affect their lives.

Long term change	How it will affect their lives
Learn to manage their money better	Fewer arguments about lack of money

PLTS in PSHE: Creative Thinkers

Teacher's Notes

Objectives

By the end of the lesson, students will:

◎   have identified creative thinking skills in other areas, including in and beyond school.

◎   have reflected on the need for creative thinking as adults within the wider community and the workplace.

Prior knowledge

Awareness of creative thinking skills as developed through previous units.

Links

Personal, Social, Health and Economic Education Programmes of Study for England: Personal Wellbeing: 1.1 Personal identities; 1.3 Risk; 1.4 Relationships.

Curriculum for Excellence for Scotland: Health and Wellbeing: Health and Wellbeing: Mental, emotional, social and physical wellbeing; Planning for choices and changes.

Personal and Social Education Framework for Wales: Preparing for lifelong learning.

Revised Curriculum for Northern Ireland: Learning for Life and Work: Personal development; Employability.

Background

This unit could be used after several of the previous units have been covered, as a way of making links between your PSHE lessons, other areas within the school and the wider community.

Starter activity

Ask students what words they associate with the phrase 'creative thinkers'. They are likely to suggest words such as 'imaginative' and 'original'. Challenge their assumptions by suggesting 'caring' (someone who thinks creatively is likely to empathise with other people), 'patient' (links with trying new solutions and follows ideas through) and 'honest' (questions own assumptions).

Activity sheets

Discuss Activity sheet **10.1 In School** to help students begin to identify examples of creative thinking. Ask them to match each picture with one or more of the creative thinking skills listed, then to suggest other examples. They can then take Activity sheet **10.2 Evidence** away with them and fill it in over a period of about a week to gather real life examples of when they are required to be creative thinkers at school. The class should compare their findings. They could use this evidence to create posters with the title 'We Are Creative Thinkers'.

Activity sheet **10.3 Beyond School** focuses on creative thinking in the wider world. Students could work through the activities in small groups before comparing ideas as a class.

Plenary

Ask students to name people they admire. These could be famous people or people they actually know. How might these people have used creative thinking skills to achieve the things they have achieved?

I wanted to take Geography but I didn't get it, so now I'll have to choose between German and History.

How can we find out what people really think about bullying in this school?

Creative thinking skills

◎ Generating ideas and exploring possibilities

◎ Asking questions to extend their thinking

◎ Connecting their own and others' ideas and experiences in inventive ways

◎ Questioning their own and others' assumptions

◎ Trying out alternatives or new solutions and following ideas through

◎ Adapting ideas as circumstances change

© Qualifications and Curriculum Authority

Let's email our link school in Turkey and ask them how they deal with the problem of litter in school.

You use the bigger wheels and I'll use the smaller, then we'll test them to see which work best.